malaysian*art*

contemporary*painting*
traditional*adornment*

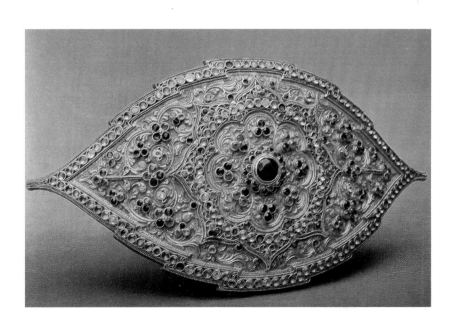

Exhibition
MALAYSIAN ART
Contemporary Painting & Traditional Adornment

Exhibition dates & venue
September 25-30, 1996
Malaysian Mission, New York U.S.A.

Publisher
Malaysia Tourism Promotion Board

Director-General
Malaysia Tourism Promotion Board
Menara Dato' Onn
Putra World Trade Centre
45, Jalan Tun Ismail
50480 Kuala Lumpur, Malaysia

Director
National Art Gallery Malaysia
No. 1 Jalan Sultan Hishamuddin
50050 Kuala Lumpur, Malaysia

Director-General
National Museum Malaysia
Jalan Damansara
50566 Kuala Lumpur, Malaysia

ISBN no. 983-9394-00-2

Exhibition organised
by Malaysia Tourism Promotion Board
and supported by National Art Gallery Malaysia and National Museum Malaysia

Contemporary Malaysian Painting
by Zainol Abidin Ahmad Shariff

Gold Jewellery and Ornaments of Malaysia, and Malaysian Songket
by Zubaidah Sual

Catalogue layout design by Abdul Raof Ahmad

Catalogue co-ordinated by National Art Gallery

Front Cover illustration Syed Ahmad Jamal, Landscape Variation
Frontispiece Pending (Belt Buckle)

The views expressed in the catalogue are not necessarily those of the publishers.

Content

Message

PRIME MINISTER
MALAYSIA

The tourism industry, apart from placing Malaysia on the world travelling map, has proved to be an important contributor to the growth of the Malaysian economy and to the well-being of our people. Revenue from our tourism industry now ranks third after manufacturing and crude petroleum and it is showing signs of even better performance over the next few years.

Culture and the Arts are developed as integral components of tourism. The Arts is an excellent medium of expression and communication, and through the arts, differences between two countries can be overcome and relationships strengthened. Friendship and understanding between artists from different countries can be further nurtured and such interaction certainly widens the perspective of Malaysian artists. Our government encourages its artists and new talents to hone their skills, extend themselves and experiment with new dimensions to produce creative and highly valued works of art by promoting their creations at home and abroad. The growing number of local and international exhibitions which focus on the arts are providing greater opportunities for our talents to explore their capabilities.

Malaysia as a developing nation has a declared objective of reaching a fully-developed and industrialised nation status by 2020. In our quest to attain this *Vision 2020*, we have not forgotten that it is essential for our people to have strong social values, including an appreciation of our heritage.

I am happy to officiate this exhibition *Malaysian Art: Contemporary Painting and Traditional Adornment*, one that reflects Malaysia's rich and multi-cultural heritage. I hope that it will give visitors, especially the American public, glimpses into Malaysian art, which in itself is a passage of information and helps broaden one's perspective of the works of expressions by Malaysian artists. I hope that this exhibition, held in such an established arts centre as vibrant as New York, will allow a better understanding of Malaysia's artistic heritage and of the Malaysian people.

Dr Mahathir bin Mohamad
Prime Minister of Malaysia

Message

منتري کبودايأان کسنيان دان فلڠچوڠن مليسيا

MENTERI KEBUDAYAAN, KESENIAN DAN PELANGCONGAN
MINISTER OF CULTURE, ARTS AND TOURISM MALAYSIA

It gives me great pleasure to say a few words in this catalogue *Malaysian Art: Contemporary Painting and Traditional Adornment* published in conjunction with an exhibition of Malaysian paintings, traditional gold ornaments and songket, in New York.

The choice of the collection is drawn from the rich and varied multi-racial heritage of Malaysia. The contemporary paintings are representative of the best works of Malaysian artists and they record the changing issues and lifestyle of a dynamic and expanding society.

The exhibition on Malaysian traditional ornaments provides a glimpse into our colourful past. Most of these objects are exquisite and unique. They are highly regarded as basic links between the past and the present. To a great extent, these national treasures have contributed to the evolution of the present Malaysian identity.

Through this exhibition, we hope modern designers can be inspired by the wealth of motifs and patterns from the past. Likewise, I hope the art collection can offer a palate of new ideas to artists in their future works. For art lovers and the public at large, this is a rare opportunity for a better understanding of Malaysian arts.

Thank you.

Dato' Sabbaruddin Chik
Minister of Culture, Arts and Tourism Malaysia

Contemporary Malaysian Painting

In 1958, a year after the country gained its independence from British colonial rule, Balai Seni Lukis Negara or the National Art Gallery of Malaysia was established in the nation's capital, Kuala Lumpur. The move by the government could be regarded not only as an indication that the country was set on moulding itself as a modern nation in a modern world, but also that the cultural significance of the practices and appreciation of contemporary art

was beginning to be recognised. By and large, the gallery is concerned with the history and development of contemporary or non-traditional art in Malaysia.

» But the gallery, by no means, *is* contemporary Malaysian art, although it has been playing a very prominent and important role in the development of that art since its inception. The beginnings of 'modern' art in Malaysia is still an open question, but current accounts have tentatively put the second decade of this century as the time when, apart from the documentary paintings of sceneries done by British colonial officials for various essentially non-aesthetic purposes, paintings alluding to European artistic idiom began to appear within Westernised social circles. Later, with the influx of immigrants fleeing the upheavals in China and looking for a better life, local exposure to Western art became widespread as some migrant Chinese artists began transferring their practices of versions of European art or Westernised Chinese art into Malayan society. These artists were invariably painters working in oils and watercolours, perhaps because the media were less cumbersome and cheaper than sculpture or printmaking. More significantly, perhaps, it was because of the kind of training and exposure they obtained in Westernised art schools in China that privileged oils for representing visual materiality. And water-based pigment on paper is of course a highly regarded traditional medium of Chinese painting. Furthermore, in the Malayan society

then, there was a small but thriving market for small-size oils and water-colours, especially amongst the wealthy Chinese merchants and entrepreneurs, whether with pretensions to Western lifestyles or traditionally Chinese, and the aspirants to cultured status among the British colonialists. And, presumably too, there were enough lovers of the art among the Malay elite and other Malayans sympathetic to European culture and lifestyles, potentially those who went to British-run schools either locally or in England.

» So, for many years contemporary art in Malaya, or 'modern art' as it was more often labelled by many who noticed its difference in form and function from 'traditional art', took to facile and direct emulations of Euro-

pean artistic idioms or to various kinds of amalgamation of European and Chinese aesthetics. Western cultural (and not just cultural) hegemony had made it oppressingly unavoidable. Those were the years when the European ways of making, seeing, evaluating and marketing art, espoused as superior by Westerners and concurred by not a few locals, were surely, but not too slowly beginning to be internalised into the modern Malaysian cultural ethos. The clearest concession to localness discernible was the subject depicted, which more often than not would be the local rural people and landscape, flora and fauna, or 'exotic' tropical pastorals. As for the mode of stylistic representations, it was the so-called 'School of Paris', or variations of it incorporating compositional devices and brushstrokes of Chinese painting traditions.

» It was not until much later that a significant attempt at giving distinct formalistic identity to the configuration of contemporary Malaysian art was made. It came in the 1950s in the form of 'batik painting', which was simply the ingenious use of traditional batik fabric printing technique to create a 'modern painting'. To many people it gave Malaysian painting an apparent and ostensible Malaysian appearance, especially when combined with the representation of scenes of rural local Malay life, as could be seen in the batik paintings of Chuah Thean Teng, a pioneer of this type of work. Curiously too, this experiment in identity formulation offers an insight into the artists' perception of modern painting. In their preoccupations with medium and technique, it could be understood that for them, modern painting was about stylistic innovations detached from considerations of meanings of subject matter. It was almost as if the figuratively represented subject was just a static matter and an excuse for artistic manipulations of the painting surface. The possibilities of meanings

top left
patrick ng kah onn
detail of menyidai kain

above
cheong lai tong
detail of nude

bottom
redza piyadasa
detail of siri malaysia no.10

of the subject depicted were not exploited enough or not addressed at all. Perhaps, it was because the artists were looking at a life from the outside. Perhaps they were not interested in the internal dynamics of the culture they were observing and representing. Perhaps that was the problem with modern painting.

» But those were not really the years of cultural and artistic insecurity, at least not for many of those in the artistic limelight. In their persistence and diligence at practising their kind of modern art, one could see a seriousness of intent and belief in the validity of their creativity within the assimilated idiom of expression. And because many of the artists were teachers, this same idiom was expounded by them in art classes, further boosting its awareness and consequently legitimising it. Of course, the ultimate legitimation of the artists was the setting up of the national gallery mentioned earlier. The only sense of insecurity some could have felt was in the anxiety of not being on par with their western counterparts, not necessarily out of a sense of cultural inferiority, but out of a sense of individual artistic professionalism. To many of the artists empathetic with the modern Western idiom, art was universal and did not have boundaries of any kind; even apolitical. Those were the Cold War years.

» Their belief in the universalism of art, however, did not mean they were oblivious to any sense of identity. On the contrary, it was precisely because of their acknowledgement of individual artistic professional integrity and their identification with the universal community of individual artists, that they became aware of the need to reflect some kind of individuality rooted in lived experiences of time and space. Understandably, with the country's attainment of sovereign independent nation status, the need to reflect that sovereignty in various aspects did not go unnoticed by them. Hence the search for national and cultural identity in its various guises since 1957.

» For many of the earlier generation of Malaysian artists, this search was not so much circumscribed by politics and national boundaries as informed by personal intimations of geo-cultural climate and sensibilities. Artists like Syed Ahmad Jamal, Yeoh Jin Leng and especially Abdul Latiff Mohidin, painters who were (and are still) very much into the abstract idiom, made allusions to the natural and cultural ambience of the Southeast Asian region rather than to any specific identification with nationality or ethnicity, even when the actual object of representation was derived from a particular physical or cultural context. Perhaps, as modernist painters they were more interested in formal aesthetic considerations than in iconography, as a result of which the specificity of the cultural

top
yeoh jin leng
detail of padi fields

above
syed ahmad jamal
detail of mandi laut

context, or identity, if you may, could mostly be read in the colours, lines, compositions and generalised (and sociologically neutralised) objects, motifs and symbols; however obscure and untenable the connection is between formal analysis and the construction of cultural identity in modernist art. They painted from and about their feelings, more than for the purpose of explicating or rationalising natural and cultural phenomena. Which is, of course, what most artists usually do, in varying degrees of intensity.

» Among the early artists who came into the public eye, one stood out conspicuously in aspiring to express cultural identity. The late Nik Zainal Abidin was unique. Before the idea of post-modernism came to give license for salvaging and appropriating traditional culture into contemporary art, he was already in the Malaysian art scene of the late 1950s through to the 1970s, unabashedly but quite innocuously transplanting almost *in toto* the cast of the traditional wayang kulit repertoire on to the modernist canvas. The wayang kulit is a tradi-

tional Malay shadow-puppet theatre form that narrates episodes from the Mahabharata and the Hikayat Seri Rama, a Malay version of the Hindu legend about Rama and Sita of the Ramayana. The paintings, however, do not tell stories, but merely present flatly-painted images of characters from the wayang, and amidst other works of painters inclined toward

similarly non-narrative Euro-American abstraction and abstract expressionism, they are unmistakably non-Western.

» Sometime in the 1970's and onwards, there was increasing concern among Malaysian artists, not just with the elusive issue of cultural identity in art, but also about addressing and connecting with social and cultural developments in the country, and outside. In their own ways, some artists began to express their reactions to what was happening around them in their artworks. With respect to this, one of the most significant developments was the fertile impact of the resurgence of the Islamic spirit in Malaysian society on the practice of contemporary art. Although, among Malay artists, there had been interest in incorporating Islamic concerns into their works earlier on, and the traditional Islamic art of calligraphy has always been alive in the hands of skilful Malay calligraphers all along, it was not until after 1980 that Islamic considerations came into the contemporary Malaysian art scene in a major way. In painting, artists like Ahmad Khalid Yusof and Sulaiman Esa are among those who consciously injected aspects into their art that they considered reflective of their Islamic concerns. The overriding thought behind the presentation of 'Islamicness' in many works of artists intent on instilling their art with Islamic spirit is the idea of *Tauhid* or Divine Unity, which they interpreted in their own way in their artworks.

» Beginning in the 1980s too, was a greater interest in traditions, new

and indigenous materials, and new forms of artistic expression and creation that transcended conventional artmaking parameters. Performance art, video art, computer art, and installation art particularly, became increasingly popular among the younger artists. Sculpture, which had never been practised much by Malaysian artists before, suddenly burst into the scene with a vengeance. This became most obvious in the Salon Malaysia 1991/92 national art competition for which the panel of judges reported that, "In one bounding leap, or so it appears, the situation has been turned on its head - at least for this occasion...". And the trend continued in the following regular Young Contemporaries art competitions. But at no time was the dominant position of painting as the most preferred art form among artists been threatened. In fact, with the increased awareness of contemporary art as attested by the mushrooming of private and corporate art galleries, the demand for painting has never been greater among the collectors, and the painters are only too glad to cater to it.

» Looking at the robust and lively state of contemporary painting in Malaysia now, it would not be wrong to conclude that there is an air of confidence in the scene; something that could not really be said about the early years, when the apparently self-conscious practice of art, in hindsight seems to be inhibited by an anxiety over the influence and control of Euro-American modernist predominance. The West today is not the sole custodian of contemporary art, nor of modernist art, for that matter.

» This exhibition attempts to present a sampling of the richness and excitement of contemporary Malaysian art. A guiding principle for the show is the obvious one of space limitation and convenience of transportation, hence the restriction to paintings of manageable sizes. As such, it does not do justice to what is actually happening in Malaysia right now. For that the visitor will need to go to Kuala Lumpur.

Zainol Abidin Ahmad Shariff
Guest Curator

Suggested readings

1. **Modern Artists of Malaysia**, by T.K.Sabapathy and Redza Piyadasa, Dewan Bahasa & Pustaka, Kuala Lumpur, 1983.

2. **Contemporary Paintings of Malaysia**, catalogue of the exhibition with the same name at the Pacific Asia Museum in Pasadena, California, June 22, 1988 - January 22, 1989.

3. **Vision and Idea, Relooking Modern Malaysian Art**, edited by T.K. Sabapathy with contributions by Krishen Jit, Redza Piyadasa, T.K. Sabapathy and Zainol Abidin Ahmad Shariff, National Art Gallery, Kuala Lumpur, 1994.

Gold Jewellery and Ornaments of Malaysia

It is believed that gold mining began in Malaysia some 2000 years ago. Foreign traders of old used to call Malaysia "The Golden Peninsula.". According to the 16th century Portuguese Chronicler Tome Pires, gold dust was found in the state of Pahang probably in the same period. There were also gold mines in other states of Peninsular Malaysia, but the yield was extremely low.

» During the early days of gold mining, the metal was obtained by the panning method. The miners used to search along the rivers using a shallow wooden dish, dipping it in and swirling the gold-bearing alluvium in the water time and again until all the sand and silt had gone, leaving the heavier gold particles as residue in the dish.

» The tools used by a local goldsmith are usually crude home-made implements. Most goldsmiths prefer to use pure gold to fashion their jewellery and ornaments because it is soft and malleable. Most jewellery however, is made from gold which has been mixed with an alloy in order to add strength, thereby reducing the cost.

Pure gold is graded as 24 karat; the lowest fold content is 10 karat. As an example, 14 karat gold has 14 parts gold to 10 parts alloy.

» The village goldsmith usually melts his gold in a small crucible using only a charcoal fire. Home-made bellows (*embusan*) keep the fire continuously glowing at a constant heat to melt the gold and the alloys evenly.

» The Chinese and Malay goldsmiths were experts in using a variety of techniques to decorate their jewellery, and produced many pieces of great aesthetic value. They were particularly adept at repousse-work and granulation techniques. Repousse-work, the art of embossing a pattern in relief

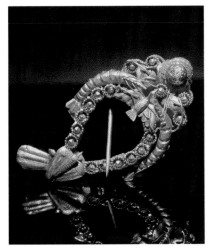

onto a thin sheet of gold, was used widely to decorate a variety of ornaments, for example, brooches (*kerosang*), dress combs (*sikat*), anklets (*gelang kaki*), belt buckles (*pending*) and weapons (*keris*).

» In some cases the ornament was composed of a number of pieces which were embossed separately, cut out, and soldered (appliquéd) together.

» Since the early days the craft of fashioning gold jewellery in Malaysia owed much to the patronage of Malay royalty, particularly in the important political centres of Kota Bharu, Kuala Terengganu and Kuala Kangsar. Skillful and talented goldsmiths gathered together in the various royal capitals where they enjoyed the luxuries afforded by royal patronage. They normally lived on the perimeter of a royal palace, or around the house of a high official. Most of their needs were supplied and they

were able to make any given object or ornament, beautiful in form and delicate in workmanship. In the days of royal patronage the court jewellers were seldom idle. Each and every item required as a personal ornament or for court ceremonies was made of gold and precious gems.

» The skill and craftsmanship of the Malay goldsmith reflect the various outside influences that have been absorbed into their techniques. Most common is the Indian influence which provides the basic functional shape. Jewellery designs of the East Coast states were also influenced by contemporary styles prevalent in Southern Thailand. Chinese styles are most evident in the states of Penang and Melaka. However, there has always been a steady interchange of ideas between Chinese and Malay craftsmen all over the Malay Peninsula. If a thorough study of the subject were to be conducted, one might observe that western influence too can be traced to quite some time back.

Zubaidah Sual
Assistant Curator
National Museum

opposite page
gelang kaki

this page
top
kerosang

above
sikat

chuah thean teng penang waterfront 1958 batik on cloth 39.2cm x 108cm **permanent collection national art gallery malaysia** 1958.3

chuah thean teng fruit season 1968 batik on cloth 87.8cm x 57.2cm **permanent collection national art gallery malaysia** 1971.17

ismail zain the marriage of sultan mansor shah 1989-91 acrylic on canvas 160cm x 130cm **private collection**

redza piyadasa siri malaysia no.10 1982 mixed media 63cm x 89cm **permanent collection national art gallery malaysia** 1984.14

nik zainal abidin wayang kulit I 1961 acrylic on board 56cm x 116cm **permanent collection national art gallery malaysia** 1993.11

nik zainal abidin durupadi 1970 watercolour on paper 87.1cm × 100.9cm **permanent collection national art gallery malaysia** 1970.1

patrick ng kah onn menyidai kain 1950 oil on canvas 50.8cm x 60.9cm permanent collection national art gallery malaysia 1959.27

patrick ng kah onn benih 1960 oil on board 99cm x 68cm **permanent collection national art gallery malaysia** 1961.8

yeoh jin leng padi fields 1963 oil on canvas 82.8cm x 102cm permanent collection national art gallery malaysia 1966.2
light reflection 1963 oil on canvas 91cm x 114cm permanent collection national art gallery malaysia 1964.35

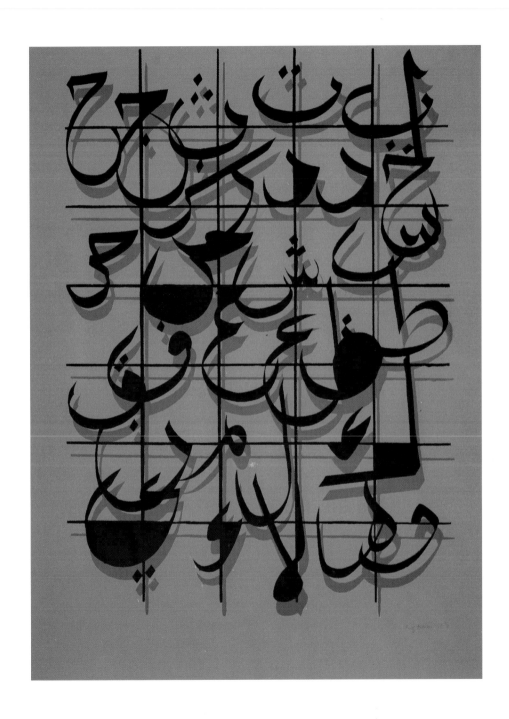

ahmad khalid yusof alif ba ta 1971 acrylic on canvas 167.6cm x 127cm **permanent collection national art gallery malaysia** 1971.5

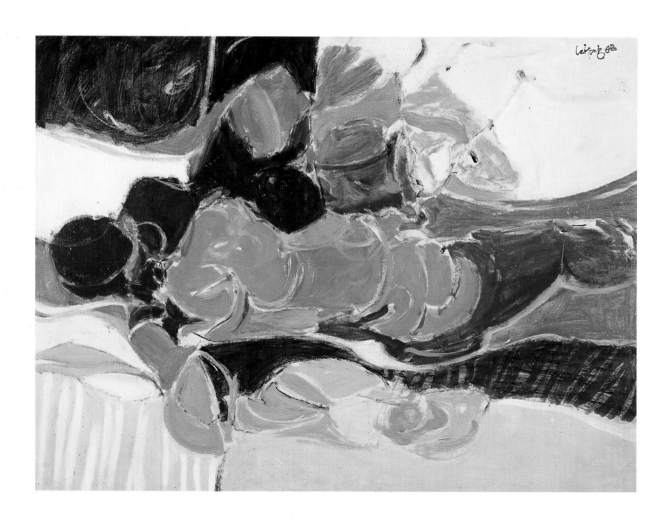

cheong lai tong nude 1968 acrylic on board 120.9cm x 90cm **permanent collection national art gallery malaysia** 1971.12

fatimah chik subuh 1995 batik on cloth 266cm x 166cm **permanent collection national art gallery malaysia** 1995.8

abdul latiff mohidin pago-pago 1964 oil on canvas 100cm × 100.3cm **permanent collection national art gallery malaysia** 1965.26

abdul latiff mohidin tumbuhan 1965 oil on canvas 81cm x 66cm **permanent collection national art gallery malaysia** 1966.2

syed ahmad jamal mandi laut (bathing in the sea) 1957 oil on board 100.5cm × 75cm permanent collection national art gallery malaysia 1969.4
landscape variation 1961 oil on board 73.8cm × 116.8cm permanent collection national art gallery malaysia 1973.26

caping (modesty disc) 6.7cm × 6.4cm 43.8grams national museum malaysia E8.1980
earrings 6.5cm 20grams national museum malaysia E36.1987

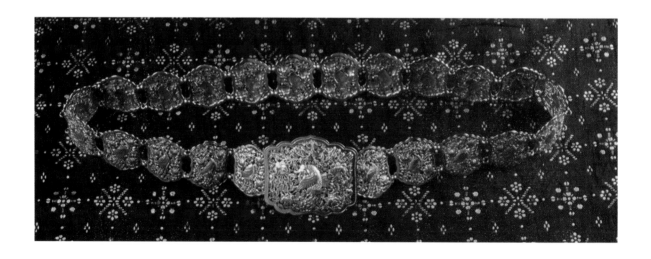

mahkota (head ornament) 17.5cm × 6.1cm 77.1grams national museum malaysia E41.1979
belt 85cm × 4cm 210grams national museum malaysia E84.1088

kerosang (brooches) 7.5cm x 3.9cm and 2.8cm 59.2grams (3) **national museum malaysia** E42/3.1979

celepa (tobacco box) 8.8cm x 5.5cm 212grams national museum malaysia E93.1971

pending (belt buckle) 22.9cm × 12cm 424.7grams national museum malaysia E132.1979

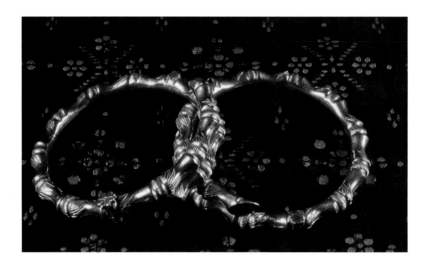

gelang tangan (bracelets) 6.2cm 34grams national museum malaysia E175.1977
cucuk sangul (hair pins) 10.5cm × 2.7cm 12.3grams national museum malaysia E192.1978

dokoh (pendant) 38.5cm × 7cm 88grams national museum malaysia E189.1977

pending (belt buckle) 8.8cm x 12.9cm 101.4grams national museum malaysia E274.1978

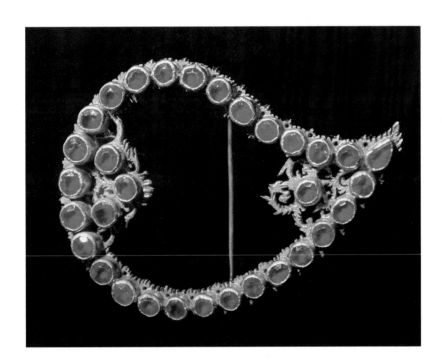

kerosang ibu (main brooch) 5cm × 7cm 37.5grams **national museum malaysia** E275.1982

bekas menghidu tembakau atau minyak wangi (snuff or scent bottle) 3.8cm x 5cm (13cm chain) 89.9grams **national museum malaysia** XI.279

gelang kaki (anklets) 12.3cm 51.2grams national museum malaysia E355.1981

dokoh (pendant) 41.8cm x 10cm 16.3grams **national museum malaysia** E311.1981

sikat (comb) 12.3cm x 3.4cm 34grams national museum malaysia E422.1980

cincin batu permata (ring with three gemstones) 2.3cm 7.95grams national museum malaysia E600.1981

dokoh (pendant) 42cm x 6.5cm 65.6grams **national museum malaysia** E991.1979

Malaysian Songket

Songket belongs to the brocade family of textiles. It is a rich, luxurious, ceremonial fabric, handwoven in silk or cotton, and intricately patterned with gold (and sometimes silver) threads which stand out in subtle relief on the background cloth. The interplay of light and gentle shadow on the fabric creates a gorgeous shimmering effect, making it undoubtedly the 'queen' of handwoven fabrics.

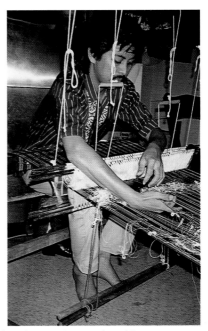

» Songket is woven on two-pedal floor looms by Malay women in the north-eastern coast of the Malay Peninsula and in Sarawak, East Malaysia. Traditionally, this songket fabric was woven in silk but today it is also woven in cotton and sometimes in a combination of both.

» Songket means inlaid gold thread or an extra weft weave, in which all warp threads are carefully counted and arranged intricately so that no overshots will appear on the right side of the fabric. Usually the traditional songket designs are very intricate and the metallic or gold threads would cover the whole fabric. Songket fabric has been used by the Malays for decoration and making costumes for ceremonial purposes for centuries. This fabric does not only have exquisite beauty but is rich in cultural values. It reflects the Malay's cultural identity through its designs and motifs as well as portrays the weaver's skillful craftsmanship.

» To weave songket, one must be very observant, imaginative and creative. The operation of a Malay loom is much the same as that in any other country. It is operated manually and one has to learn the correct method if one is to set up the loom and to weave songket. Most of the songket pattern designs are in transversely symmetric style, especially on a full-patterned songket.

» A good woven songket is judged by looking at the neatness of the weaving and at the selvedge of the fabric.

» The beauty of songket lies in its intricate design and the motifs produced on the handwoven cloth. There are more than a hundred traditional motifs which could be found in the *kain songket sarong* as well as *kain lepas songket* or *selendang songket*.

» Motifs and patterns in songket were mostly inspired from the natural environment such as flowers, mountains, the sea and the sky.

» Songket materials are used as dress fabrics and for furnishings such as cushion covers, placemats, decorative wall hangings and gift items. Today songket patterns are used to decorate buildings, greeting cards and stamps, and evidently are popular in Malaysian textile design too because they are symbolic of the Malay cultural heritage.

Zubaidah Sual
Assistant Curator
National Museum

acclaimed songket weaver
hafshin bin abdul aziz
experience 15 years in songket making
achievement awarded a prize for creativity in traditional textile design by Terengganu state government 1989

List of Artworks

National Art Gallery Malaysia

Chuah Thean Teng
Penang Waterfront, 1958, Batik on cloth, 39.2cm x 108 cm
Permanent Collection 1958.3

Chuah Thean Teng
Fruit Season, 1968, Batik on cloth, 87.8cm x 57.2 cm
Permanent Collection 1971.17

Ismail Zain
The Marriage of Sultan Mansor Shah, 1989-91, Acrylic on canvas, 160cm x 130 cm
Private Collection

Ismail Zain
Saradha, 1983, Acrylic on canvas and collage, 122cm x 92 cm
Private Collection

Nik Zainal Abidin
Wayang Kulit 1 (Shadow Puppet Theatre 1), 1961, Acrylic on board, 56cm x 116 cm
Permanent Collection 1993.11

Nik Zainal Abidin
Durupadi, 1970, Watercolour on paper, 87.1cm x 100.9 cm
Permanent Collection 1970.1

Patrick Ng Kah Onn
Menyidai Kain (Drying Clothes), 1950, Oil on canvas, 50.8cm x 60.9 cm
Permanent Collection 1959.27

Patrick Ng Kah Onn
Benih (Seed), 1960, Oil on board, 99cm x 68 cm
Permanent Collection 1961.8

Redza Piyadasa
Siri Malaysia No. 10 (Malaysian Series No.10), 1982, Mixed media, 63cm x 89 cm
Permanent Collection 1984.14

Redza Piyadasa
Malay Wedding Couple, 1988, Mixed media and collage, 55cm x 45 cm
Private Collection

Sulaiman Hj. Esa
Nurani (Light), 1983, Hand-made paper, yarn, & bamboo, 150cm x 150 cm
Permanent Collection 1984.8

Syed Ahmad Jamal
Mandi Laut (Bathing in the Sea), 1957, Oil on board, 100.5cm x 75 cm
Permanent Collection 1959.4

Syed Ahmad Jamal
Landscape Variation, 1961, Oil on board, 73.8cm x 116.8 cm
Permanent Collection 1973.26

Abdul Latiff Mohidin
Pago-Pago, 1964, Oil on canvas, 100cm x 100.3 cm
Permanent Collection 1965.26

Abdul Latiff Mohidin
Tumbuhan (Plants), 1965, Oil on canvas, 81cm x 66cm
Permanent Collection 1966.2

Yeoh Jin Leng
Padi Fields, 1963, Oil on canvas, 82.8cm x 102 cm
Permanent Collection 1963.40

Yeoh Jin Leng
Light Reflection, 1963, Oil on canvas, 91cm x 114 cm
Permanent Collection 1964.35

Ibrahim Hussein
Why you are the way you are, 1969, Mixed media, 195.6cm x 121.9 cm
Permanent Collection 1981.48

Ahmad Khalid Yusof
Alif Ba Ta, 1971, Acrylic on canvas, 167.6cm x 127 cm
Permanent Collection 1971.5

Cheong Lai Tong
Nude, 1968, Acrylic on board, 120cm x 90 cm
Permanent Collection 1971.12

Fatimah Chik
Subuh (Dawn), 1995, Batik, 266cm x 166 cm
Permanent Collection 1995.8

National Museum Malaysia

Snuff Bottle, XI.279

Head Ornament, E41.1979

Pendant, E189.1977

Breast Ornament, E1034.1979

Pendant, E1053.1979

Belt Buckle, E132.1979

Belt Buckle, E133.1979

Belt, E238.1982

Brooches, E72.1984

Tobacco Box, E93.1971

Ring, E600.1981

Ring, E1000.1979

Earstud, E1054. 1979

Earring, E297.1978

Brooches, E42.1979

Anklets, E355.1981

Comb, E422.1980

Comb, E421.1980

Belt Buckle, E239.1981

Belt Buckle, E274.1978

Hair Pins, E367.1979

Charm Bracelet, E318. 1982

Pendant, E991.1979

Anklets, E107.1980

Belt, E306.1982

Bracelets, E175.1977

Modesty Disc, E8.1980

Hair Pins, E192, E193, E194.1978

Modesty Disc, E211.1977

Modesty Disc, E289.1982

Brooch, E275.1982

Belt, E84.1988

Necklace, E311.1981

Hair Pins, E92.1988

Earring, E36.1987

Bangle, NM 1996

Bracelet, NM 1996

Ring, E607.1987

Necklace, E32.1987

Belt Buckle, E311.1982

Acknowledgement

The Chairman and staff of the Malaysia Tourism Promotion Board are indebted to the following for making this exhibition possible :

The Right Honourable Dato' Seri Dr. Mahathir Mohamad, Prime Minister, Malaysia.

The Honourable Dato' Sabbaruddin Chik, Minister of Culture, Arts and Tourism Malaysia.

H.E. Dato' Hashim Dali, Ambassador of Malaysia to the United States of America.

H.E. Tan Sri Razali Ismail, Permanent Representative of Malaysia to the United Nations and Puan Sri Diane Razali.

H.E. Mr. Livia S. Sylva, Commissioner of the New York City Commission for the United Nations and Consular Corporations.

Dr. Kamarul Baharin bin Buyong, Director General, Department of Museums and Antiquity Malaysia.

Puan Wairah Marzuki, Director, National Art Gallery, Malaysia

and all who have contributed in one way or another to the success of this project.